HARDPRESS.NET
HOME OF HARD-TO-FIND BOOKS

The Nests at Washington, and Other Poems
by John James Piatt

No subject

S, Davis

THE NESTS AT WASHINGTON,

AND

OTHER POEMS.

BY

JOHN JAMES PIATT,

AND

SARAH M. (BRYAN) PIATT.

NEW YORK,

WALTER LOW, 823 BROADWAY.

LONDON: SAMPSON LOW, SON & CO.

1864.

Entered according to Act of Congress, in the year 1863,

By WALTER LOW,

the Clerk's Office of the District Court of the United States for the
Southern District of New York.

A. ALVORD, ELECTROTYPER AND PRINTER.

TO

JAMES RUSSELL LOWELL.

TO GIVE YOUR NAME AN HONOR I WERE FAIN,
  BUT—THOUGH WITH A RICH WILL—I ONLY MAKE
MY POOR DEED PROUD BEARING YOUR NAME IN VAIN:
  I CANNOT GIVE THE HONOR THAT I TAKE.

J. J. P.

WOODLEY, GEORGETOWN HEIGHTS, D. C.,
    October, 1863.

CONTENTS.

5

CONTENTS.

II.

I.

J. J. D.

THE STRANGE ORGANIST.

DEEP in the dim cathedral gloom,
   Where incense all the ages rose,
I walk, alone.   The mystic bloom
   Of saintly silence round me glows.

High Church of Song !   O hallow'd place,
   Where haunt the hymns of bards of old !
Light shone on many a lifted face
   When holy floods of music roll'd.

Deep in the dim cathedral hush
   I stand alone, the Organ's keys
Touching with wandering fingers—blush,
   Sad soul, what harmonies are these !

THE NESTS AT WASHINGTON.

BEFORE the White House portals,
　　The careless eyes behold
Three iron bombs uplifted,
　　Adusk in summer gold.

In dreamy mood I wander'd
　　At Sabbath sunset there,
While the wide city's murmur
　　Hummed vaguely everywhere:

" Black seeds of desolation,"
　　I said, " by War's red hand
Sown in the fierce sirocco
　　Over the wasted Land !

" Unholy with the holy,
　　What do ye here to-day,
Symbols of awful battle,
　　In Sabbath's peaceful ray ?"

11

THE NESTS AT WASHINGTON.

Angel of Dust and Darkness !
  I heard thy woeful breath,
With noise of all earth's battles,
  Answer: " Let there be Death!"

I thought of many a midnight,
  Where sprang terrific light
Over wide woods and marshes;
  Fierce fire-flies lit the night.

I saw beleaguer'd bastions
  Leap up in red dismay,
Wide rivers all transfigured
  Awake in dreadful day.

Asleep in peaceful sunshine
  Glimmer'd the warlike things :
Into their hollow horror
  Flew tenderest summer wings !

Deep in the awful chambers
  Of the gigantic Death,
The wrens their nests had builded
  And dwelt with loving breath.

12

THE NESTS AT WASHINGTON.

Angel of Resurrection!
Over all buried strife
I heard thy bird-song whisper,
Sweetly, " Let there be Life !"

WASHINGTON, D. C., June, 1862.

2   13

WESTERN WINDOWS.

CRIMSONING the woodlands dumb and hoary,
  Bleak with long November winds and rains,
Lo, at sunset, breathes a sudden glory,
  Breaks a fire on all the western panes.

Eastward far I see the restless splendor
  Shine through many a window-lattice bright
Nearer all the farmhouse gables render
  Flame for flame and melt in breathless light.

Many a mansion, many a cottage lowly,
  Lost in radiance, palpitate the same
At the touch of Beauty strange and holy,
  All transfigured in the evening flame.

Luminous, within—a marvellous vision—
  Things familiar half-unreal show ;
In the effluence of Land Elysian,
  Every bosom feels a holier glow.

14

Faces lose, as at some wondrous portal,
   Earthly masks, and heavenly features wear :
Many a mother, like a saint immortal,
   Folds her child, a halo'd angel fair.

THE LOST HORIZON.

I STOOD at evening in the crimson air:
    The trees shook off their dusky twilight glow;
The wind took up old burdens of despair,
    And moan'd like Atlas with his world of woe.

Like the great circle of a bronzed ring,
    That clasp'd the vision of the vanish'd day,
I saw the vague horizon vanishing
    Around me into darkness, far away.

Then, while the night came fast with cloudy roar,
    Lo, all about me, rays of hearths unknown
Sprang from the gloom with light unseen before,
    And made a warm horizon of their own.

I sigh'd: " The wanderer in the desert sees
    Strange ghosts of summer lands arising, sweet
With restless waters, green with gracious trees
    Whose shadows beckon welcome to his feet.

THE LOST HORIZON.

"For erst, where now the desert far away
    Stretches a wilderness of hopeless sand,
Clasping fair fields and sunburnt harvests lay
    The heavenly girdles of a fruitful land."

I thought of a sweet mirage now no more:
    Warm windows radiant with a dancing flame—
Dear voices heard within a happy door—
    A face that to the darkness, lighted, came.

No hearth of mine was waiting, near or far;
    No threshold for my coming footstep yearn'd
To touch its slumber; no warm window star,
    The tender Venus, to my longing burn'd.

The darken'd windows slowly lost their fire,
    But shimmer'd with the ghostly ember-light:
A wanderer, with old embers of desire,
    The lost horizon held me in the night.

THE DARK STREET.

O WEARY feet that fill the nightly air!
  No hearts I hear, no faces see above—
I feel your single yearning, everywhere,
  Moving the way of Love!

Forever crowding weary, one by one
  Ye pass no more through all the shadowy air;
The footsteps cease on thresholds dearly lone—
  The hearts, the faces there!

There all the voices of the heart arise,
  Unheard along the darkling street before;
The faces light their loving lips and eyes—
  The footsteps are no more!

18

APART.

At sea are tossing ships;
　On shore are dreaming shells.
And the waiting heart and the loving lips,
　Blossoms and bridal bells.

At sea are sails a-gleam;
　On shore are longing eyes,
And the far horizon's haunting dream
　Of ships that sail the skies.

At sea are masts that rise
　Like spectres from the deep;
On shore are the ghosts of drowning cries
　That cross the waves of sleep.

At sea are wrecks a-strand;
　On shore are shells that moan,
Old anchors buried in barren sand,
　Sea-mist and dreams alone.

THE MASTER-KEY.

Lo! in my lifted hand a little Key:
  What matter if of iron or of gold,
My simplest gift, my greatest gift, you see;
  My life, Beloved, when it is given you hold.

Enter whene'er you choose: at vesper chime,
  Or when the dewy lips of midnight, dumb,
Kiss the dumb world. Behold, at morning's prime
  My doors are open, and the many come.

The many come—it matters little who:
  I guard the place and welcome, evermore.
My sacred chambers, never closed to you,
  Are closed for them: I keep the outer door.

Enter whene'er you will, for every room
  Is yours in being mine. To you unknown,
This Key knows outward porch and inner gloom,
  Each sky-ward stair, each closet dim and lone.

THE MASTER-KEY.

Dance in the echoing halls, Beloved, and sing
   Away your heart to every echo sweet
(The echoes, too, are mine), with flitting wing
   Of buoyant joy and scarce-alighting feet.

The lighted walls shall answer your delight,
   With floating shapes and summer dreams of Art
The Undine springing from her fountain bright,
   The lithe Baccanthé with her panting heart.

Dream in the purple glooms, for dreaming made,
   Where the white angel holds the lily white
Against her marble bosom (in the shade
   Her wings forgotten), watching day and night.

What though at times along the floors—unknown,
   Unheard by others—echo phantom feet,
Weird faces start from veils, faint voices moan?
   Know Life and Death in every passage meet.

Open the chambers where the unburied dead,
   While Memory there forever wakeful stands,
Show their thin ghostly radiance not yet fled—
   Pure breathless faces, tender folded hands.

THE MASTER-KEY.

Around the death-beds, hush'd, familiar go,
 And kiss for me the dear familiar clay,
While the dark funeral tapers waver slow
 And the old death-watch is renew'd for aye.

Walk in my secret chapel when you will:
 Lo! Visions come adown some unseen stair;
Sometimes high voices all the silence fill,
 And St. Cecilia's soul is in the air.

Fear not: the angel with the lily white
 There watches, too, as in the dreaming place,
With wings uplifted in mysterious light
 And some white morning on her lifted face.

Enter, whene'er you choose, whatever door:
 This Key will open, night and day, the whole.
Be Love with you, your guardian evermore;
 Fear nothing. Take the Master of my Soul.

22

AT CHRISTMAS EVE.

I saw the tide of Christmas
   Within the darkness rise:
It flow'd in the hearts of the children,
   And leap'd in their loving eyes.

The windows breathed the splendor
   Of the joyous day at hand;
In the rainy streets of the city
   Shone visions of Fairy-Land.

There were ships and cars and houses,
   Built marvelously well;
Fruits from the Tropics of Fancy,
   And flowers of Miracle!

There were picture-books of enchantment:
   Gems from the wonder-mines;
The ark with the world's old family,
   And myriad new designs.

AT CHRISTMAS EVE.

There were birds and beasts unnumber'd,
    Unnamed by me, I am sure;
And, wearing many costumes,
    The world in miniature.

" Many a Tree of Christmas
    Is loaded with joy to-night ;
Many a bough shall blossom,
    Enchanted, at morning light !"

I said, and thought of the children,
    In many a dancing home,
For the Angel of Christmas waiting
    And longing for him to come.

" They press their joyous faces
    Against the darken'd pane,
And the lighted world behind them
    They see without in the rain !"

I said, and thought of the children,
    Abroad in the street at night,
Who know no Angel of Christmas
    By gifts at morning light:

AT CHRISTMAS EVE.

" They press their saddened faces
 Against the lighted pane
And the darken'd world behind them
 They feel, without in the rain !"

3   25

THE BRONZE STATUE—APRIL, 1861.

UPLIFTED when the April sun was down,
Gold-lighted by the tremulous, fluttering beam,
Touching his glimmering steed with spurs in gleam,
The Great Virginia Colonel into town
Rode, with the scabbard, emptied, on his thigh,
The Leader's hat upon his head, and lo !
The old still manhood in his face aglow,
And the old generalship up in his eye !
" O father !" said I, speaking in my heart,
" Though but thy bronzéd form is ours alone,
And marble lips here in thy chosen place,
Rides not thy spirit in to keep thine own,
Or weeps thy Land, an orphan in the mart ?"
The twilight dying lit the deathless face.

WASHINGTON, D. C.

THE FIRST FIRE.

Dearest, to-night upon our Hearth
   See the first fire of Autumn leap:
Oh, first that we with festal Mirth
   For loving Memory keep !
Sweet Fairy of the Fireside, come
And guard our altar-flame of Home !

Without, October breathes the night—
   Cold dews below, cold stars on high ;
The chilly cricket sees our light
   Reach welcoming arms anigh,
And sighs to sing his evening song
In our warm air the winter long.

Blithe cricket ! welcome, singing, here !
   I half-recall dead Autumns cold,
With half-shut eyelids dream, my dear,
   Their sadness vague and old :
Ha ! the lithe flame leaps red, and tries
With bursting sparks to blind my eyes !

THE FIRST FIRE.

Ill-timed the gay conceit, I know:
   On the dark hills that near us lie
(The Shadow will not, need not, go)
   Beneath the Autumnal sky
Stand battle-tents, that, everywhere,
Keep ghostly white the moonless air.

The sentinel walks his lonely beat,
   The soldier slumbers on the ground:
To one hearth-glimmers far are sweet,
   One dreams of fireside sound!
From unforgotten doors they reach,
Dear sympathies, as dear as speech.

I think of all the homeless woe,
   The battle-winter long;
Alas, the world——the hearth's aglow!
   And, hark! the cricket's song
Within!—the Fairy's minstrel sings
Away the ghosts of saddest things!

The firelight strikes our walls to bloom—
   Home's tender warmth in flower, I deem:
And look, the pictures in the room
   Shine in the restless gleam—
Dear, humble fancies of the heart
When Art was Love in love with Art:

THE FIRST FIRE.

The Torrent lost in rainbow spray;
  The Flock (its shepherdess the moon)
Asleep; the Laureate-Lark of Day
  At home some even in June;
The Window, wide for beam and bee:
A dove within—without, the sea!

A Cottage in a summer land,
  With one whose shadow walks before
Snow-peaks afar in sunset stand—
  Vines flutter at the door,
Half-hiding in a sunlit place,
But cannot hide, a sunlit face;

The Mother, with her arms about
  Her baby kiss'd from evening sleep—
Still rocks the cradle: laugh and shout
  Within her bosom keep
Glad echoes—on her drooping hair
A sunbeam, 'lighting, lingers there;

The Angel visiting her Child,
  Hovering with a yearning grace,
Flush'd by the firelight, sweetly mild,
  A mother's brooding face:
Her wings (the boy has dreaming eyes)
Show that she came from Paradise!

THE FIRST FIRE.

Blithe dance the flames and blest are we!
  Without, the funeral of the year
Is preach'd by every mournful tree;
  The tree in blossom here
Knows no lost leaves, no vanish'd wing—
In vain will Autumn preach to Spring!

The cricket sings.   His song?   You know:
  Warm prophecies of dearest days—
(Horizons lost of long ago
  Crumble within the blaze!)
Of nights aglow with lights that bless
And wine from Home's enchanted press.

The cricket sings; and, as I dream,
  Your face shows tender smile and tear—
What angels of the hearth, a-gleam,
  Wingless, have lighted here?
Sing, cricket, sing of these to-night—
The First Fire of our Home is bright!

GEORGETOWN, D. C., October, 1861.

TWO PATRONS.

"WHAT shall I sing," I sigh'd and said,
  "That men shall know me when my name
Is lost with kindred lips and dead
  Are laurels of familiar fame?"

Below, a violet in the dew
  Breathed through the dark its vague perfume
Above, a star in quiet blue
  Touch'd with a gracious ray the gloom.

"Sing, friend, of me," the violet sigh'd,
  "That I may haunt your grave with love;"
"Sing, friend, of me," the star replied,
  "That I may light the dark above."

31

A MIRAGE OF THE WEST.

ABOVE the sunken sun the clouds are fired
With a dark splendor: the enchanted hour
Works momentary miracles in the sky;
Weird shadows take from fancy what they lack
For semblance, and I see a boundless plain,
A mist of sun and sheaves in boundless air,
Gigantic shapes of Reapers moving slow
In some new harvest: so I can but dream
Of my great Land, that takes its Morning star
Out of the dusky Evening of the East,
My Land, that lifted into vision gleams
Misty and vast, a boundless plain afar,
(Like yonder fading fantasy of cloud,)
With shadowy Reapers moving, vague and slow,
In some wide harvest of the days to be—
A mist of sun and sheaves in boundless air!

THE BLACKBERRY FARM.

NATURE gives with freëst hands
Richest gifts to poorest lands:
When the lord has sown his last
And his field 's to desert pass'd,
She begins to claim her own,
And—instead of harvests flown,
Sunburnt sheaves and golden ears—
Sends her hardier pioneers;
Barbarous brambles, outlaw'd seeds,
The first families of weeds
Fearing neither sun nor wind,
With the flowers of their kind
(Outcasts of the garden-bound),
Colonize the expended ground,
Using (none her right gainsay)
Confiscations of decay:
Thus she clothes the barren place,
Old disgrace, with newer grace.
Title-deeds, which cover lands
Ruled and reap'd by buried hands,

THE BLACKBERRY FARM.

She—disowning owners old,
Scorning their "to have and hold"—
Takes herself; the mouldering fence
Hides with her munificence;
O'er the crumbled gatepost twines
Her proprietary vines;
On the doorstep of the house
Writes in moss "Anonymous,"
And, that beast and bird may see,
"This is Public property;"
To the bramble makes the sun
Bearer of profusion:
Blossom-odors breathe in June
Promise of her later boon,
And in August's brazen heat
Grows the prophecy complete—
Lo, her largess glistens bright,
Blackness diamonded with light!
Then, behold, she welcomes all
To her annual festival:
"Mine the fruit but yours as well,"
Speaks the Mother Miracle;
"Rich and poor are welcome; come,
Make to-day millennium
In my garden of the sun:
Black and white to me are one.

THE BLACKBERRY FARM.

This my freehold use content—
Here no landlord rides for rent;
I proclaim my jubilee,
In my Black Republic, free.
Come," she beckons; " Enter, through
Gates of gossamer, doors of dew
(Lit with Summer's tropic fire),
My Liberia of the brier."

GEORGETOWN HEIGHTS, July, 1863.

THE MONK'S VISION OF CHRIST.

BEHOLD, unto a monk the vision grew
   Of Him who waits for all, his loving Lord,
Him who, all-suffering, all patience knew,
   And wore the crown of Hate for Love's reward.

The perfect vision of most holy light,
   The Guest of man, unto His follower dear,
Gave (He who gave the blind his mortal sight)—
   Immortal light to see his Master near.

Long gazed the monk; his rapture grew the more:
   The Sight remained, nor grew his soul content,
Till in his heart a message from the poor,
   Fed by his bounty, whisper'd, and he went.

His duty called, Christ's own belovéd care,
   While, in his room, Christ seem'd himself to
      stay;
But Christ was in his heart: so, keeping there
   The vision sweet, he walk'd his Master's way.

THE MONK'S VISION OF CHRIST.

He walked His Way, fulfilling, as he went,
  His Master's word and unforgotten will:
Returning—heaven-rewarded, self-content—
  Lo, the dear vision waited for him still!

"Thy Will be done," in many a prayer before
  His heart had lifted. Lo, the Vision said
(His Will being done who visits still the poor)
  Lowly: "Hadst thou remain'd, I must have fled."

4   87

PARTING.

We clasp our hands : we turn and go,
   Our footsteps echoing years between ;
We meet again : we hardly know
   These ghosts of loved ones long unseen.

We clasp our hands : we turn and go,
   Far travellers with strange hours and years
The face, the form, the voice we know,
   They come not back from time and tears.

We clasp our hands in loving trust ;
   We send our voices o'er the wave :
No hand can reach us—from the dust ;
   No voice can find us—in the grave.

ANTAEUS.

AWEARY of the restless will to know
Invisible heights, which men have sigh'd to reach,
And walk the deep sea, without faith, alone,
I thought of that lithe wrestler, born of Earth,
Who strove with him the hydra's conqueror,
Losing and winning.   Lifted into air
He swoon'd defeated: touching then the sod,
His blood sprang full of wings and he arose,
The heaving pulses of the hills his own,
The sinews of the deserts in his thighs.
And, when I fell asleep at middle night,
My thought becoming portion of my sleep,
I wander'd into Libyan solitudes
(For so a dream confuses place and time)
And to me spake the giant of the Waste:
"I am Antaeus, darling of the Earth.
Whatever makes me stronger, man, is thine;
I am a man, but these ungirded arms,
Forever striving, writhe forever more,
Wrestling with gods and godlike challengers.
Born of the Earth, I cling to her for strength,

ANTAEUS.

Her life is mine and mine is hers forever;
I feel my thews alone when standing fast,
A brother of the mountains, at their feet,
And dare to know my conquerors: they dwell
Aloft in myriad shapes and essences;
Sometimes they wait and seize me, unaware,
In whirlwinds of white frenzy, and I fall
Weak as a leaf whose last breath is gone out
In the first breath of Autumn: waking, then,
(Like one who, falling, wakens from his dream,)
I see a wingéd giant near the sun.
I know my place, my victors know their own:
Theirs the invisible Æther, mine below
Where the Earth breathes her breath, a breath of
      Life,
And if perchance I clasp them in my arms
Victorious here, I claim them as my own,
Servants of men and wingéd messengers.
   "I am Antaeus, darling of the Earth,
Wrestler with gods and godlike challengers,
But, oftentimes, aweary of my strife,
And of the clasp of those invisible arms,
Ready to catch and lift me up in swoon,
The death-in-life that I alone can know,
And weary of the wrestlers coming still
With challenges in the air, for rest I turn

ANTAEUS.

To the dear bosom of my Mother Earth:
She, like a mother, holds me near her heart;
She, like a mother, kisses me asleep
On loving pillows hush'd for harmless dreams;
She, like a mother, with a mother's voice
At morning wakens me.   Dear Mother Earth,
Dearest and tenderest Mother, quick with love,
Throbbing with vigor, full of gentleness,
I give myself to thee, and thou dost give
Thyself to me again; thy weary child,
Asleep upon thy bosom, wakens strong,
For thou awakest in my heart anew,
Rising immortal in my mortal strength."
  It was a voice and pass'd, as voices pass
From dreams but leave a wake of sound—a form
And vanish'd, leaving something for the sight,
Shadowy and vast, the shadow of a shade;
And I awoke, and o'er my head a vine
Bronzed with an early splendor, to and fro
A playful breeze within my window caught;
I heard the noise of morning; far away
I saw a ploughman, and a sower near
Dropp'd corn into his furrows, trusting still
All golden promises of growing gain;
And when I walk'd abroad my shadow made
A giant's bulk, my sunburnt breast beat full

ANTAEUS.

Of the great blood which moved in giants' veins
When, as we speak, the Earth itself was young;
And, while I saw an engine drag its world,
And watch'd an eagle in his azure deeps,
I smiled at the vague medley of my dream,
But said, "I am Antaeus, born of Earth,
Her chosen wrestler; lifted into air
I swoon defeated: touching then the sod,
My blood springs full of wings and I am strong."

ROSE AND ROOT.

A FABLE OF TWO LIVES.

THE Rose aloft in sunny air,
  Beloved alike by bird and bee,
Takes for the dark Root little care,
  That toils below it ceaselessly.

I put my question to the flower :
  " Pride of the Summer, garden-queen,
Why livest thou thy little hour ?"
  And the Rose answer'd, " I am seen."

I put my question to the Root—
  "I mine the earth content," it said,
" A hidden miner underfoot ;
  I know a Rose is overhead."

48

THE BURIED ORGAN.

FAR in a valley green and lone,
    Lying within some legend old,
Sometimes is heard an Organ's tone,
    Trembling, into the silence roll'd :
In vanish'd years (the legend stands)
    To save it from the unhallowing prey
Of foeman's sacrilegious hands,
    The monks their Organ bore away.

None knows the spot wherein they laid
    That body of the heavenly soul
Of Music : deep in forest shade,
    Forgotten, lies the grave they stole ;
But oftentimes, in Morning gold,
    Or through the Twilight's hushing air,
Within that valley, green and old,
    The Organ's soul arises there.

THE BURIED ORGAN.

Oh, low and sweet, and strange, and wild,
   It whispers to the holier air,
Gentle as lispings of a child—
   Mild as a mother's breathless prayer
While silence trembles, sweet and low:
   Then rapture bursts into the skies,
And chanting angels, winging slow
   On wings of music, seem to rise!

The herdsman sometimes, all alone,
   Within that haunted place is lost:
He hears the buried Organ's tone—
   His breath is prayer, his hands are cross'd!
And, while into his heart it steals,
   With hushing footsteps, downcast eyes,
Some grand cathedral's awe he feels—
   A church of air, and earth, and skies!

Often, when the sweet wand of Spring
   Has fill'd the woods with flowers unsown,
Or Autumn's dreamy breeze's wing
   Flutters through falling leaves, alone
I wander forth, and leave behind
   The city's dust, the sultry glow:
A lonely dell, far-off, I find—
   The Buried Organ 's there, I know!

THE BURIED ORGAN.

Within the city's noisy air
  I leave the creeds their Sabbath bells;
I cross my hands, my breath is prayer,
  Hearing that Organ's mystic swells.
The sweet birds sing, the soft winds blow,
  The flowers have whispers low, apart:
All wake within me, loud or low,
  God's buried Organ—in my heart!

46

QUATRAINS.

THE MICROSCOPE AND TELESCOPE.

Look down into the Microscope, and know
 The boundless wonder in the hidden small;
Look up into the Telescope, and, lo !
 The hidden greatness in the boundless all !

A DIAL AT A GRAVE.

To number sunny hours by shadows, why
 Is here the dial shown,
Where from the Sunshine of Eternity
 The Shadow, Time, is flown ?

THE HIPPOGRIFF.

Spurn not Life's calls—though seeking higher
  things—
 Earth's loving fires for the celestial levin :
The hippogriff has feet as well as wings,
 For highways of the world and paths of heaven.

QUATRAINS.

TO THE SUN.

FLOWER-WAKENER, that wakest the spheres in light.
  I worship thee alike in joy or sorrow:
Thou leavest behind thee the Eternal Night,
  Thou bear'st before thee the Eternal Morrow.

FOR———, A POET.

To own a quarry proves no call of Art—
  'T is Nature's store you cannot keep nor give,
If at your touch the masses will not start,
  Radiant processions, shapes that breathe and live !

TORCH-LIGHT IN AUTUMN.

I LIFT this sumach-bough with crimson flare
  And, touch'd with subtle pangs of dreamy pain,
Through the dark wood a torch I seem to bear
    In Autumn's funeral train.

48

THE LAST FIRE.

THE First Fire, one remember'd night
Of chilly fall, we kindled : bright
       And beautiful were its gleams !
Warming the new world all our own
And welcoming radiant futures, shone
       That prophecy of our dreams !

Our window buried against the cold,
And faces from the dark, behold !
       In transient haloes came ;
The household troubadour of mirth,
The cricket, took with song our hearth
       And bless'd the blessing flame.

O flushing firelight, rosy-warm !
O walls with many a floating form
       Of dreamy shade a-bloom !
Fancy, by Love transfigured, wrought
All miracles of tender thought,
       Transfiguring the room !

THE LAST FIRE.

Beloved and bless'd and beautified,
God-given, Angel by my side !
        The winter came and went,
And never, since the world began,
Grew sweeter happiness to man,
        Or tenderer content.

At dawn we leave the place, so warm
And bright with you December's storm
        Nor cold nor shadow brought :
The Last Fire warms our walls to-night ;
The window breathes its wonted light,
        But sadness haunts our thought.

By tenderest tides of feeling stirr'd
Your heart brings tears for every word :
        I hear you murmur low,
" Here blossom'd Home for you and me—
Love walk'd without his glamoury
        And stood diviner so.

" Dear echoes, answering day by day—
We cannot take the past away !
        The threshold and the floor,
Where Love's familiar steps have been
Repeated evermore within,
        Are dear forever more !"

THE LAST FIRE.

Yes, but the place beloved shall be
Bequeath'd to loving Memory :
       The spirits of the place,
The Larés of the household air,
Born of the heart, the heart must bear—
       They know no stranger's face.

The atmosphere we fill is ours :
It moves with us its sun and showers ;
       It is our world alone,
Vivid with all our souls create,
The plastic dream, the stone of Fate—
       We take and keep our own.

So let the Last Fire flame and fall,
The ghostly ember-shadows crawl,
       The ashes fill the hearth :
The cricket travels where we go,
And Home is but the Heaven below
       Transfiguring the Earth !

THE GRAVE-ANGEL.

In the moonlight, on the tombstone,
  Stands the Sculptor's marble dream
From its face its soul is lifted,
  And its wings soul-lifted seem.

On the tombstone stands the Angel,
  And its left hand points below ;
To its lips is press'd a finger :
  'T is the Angel Death, I know.

52

THE MORNING STREET.

Alone I walk the Morning Street,
Fill'd with the silence vague and sweet:
All seems as strange, as still, as dead
As if unnumber'd years had fled,
Letting the noisy Babel lie
Breathless and dumb against the sky;
The light wind walks with me alone
Where the hot day flame-like was blown,
Where the wheels roar'd, the dust was beat
The dew is in the Morning Street.

Where are the restless throngs that pour
Along this mighty corridor
While the noon shines?—the hurrying crow
Whose footsteps make the city loud—
The myriad faces—hearts that beat
No more in the deserted street?
Those footsteps in their dreaming maze
Cross thresholds of forgotten days;
Those faces brighten from the years

THE MORNING STREET.

In rising suns long set in tears;
Those hearts—far in the Past they beat,
Unheard within the Morning Street.

A city of the world's gray prime,
Lost in some desert far from Time,
Where noiseless ages, gliding through,
Have only sifted sand and dew—
Yet a mysterious hand of man
Lying on all the haunted plan,
The passions of the human heart
Quickening the marble breast of Art—
Were not more strange to one who first
Upon its ghostly silence burst
Than this vast quiet where the tide
Of Life, upheav'd on either side,
Hangs trembling, ready soon to beat
With human waves the Morning Street.

Ay, soon the glowing morning flood
Breaks through the charméd solitude:
This silent stone, to music won,
Shall murmur to the rising sun;
The busy place, in dust and heat,
Shall rush with wheels and swarm with feet

THE MORNING STREET.

The Arachné-threads of Purpose stream
Unseen within the morning gleam;
The life shall move, the death be plain;
The bridal throng, the funeral train,
Together, face to face shall meet
And pass within the Morning Street.

THE DESERTED SMITHY.

At the end of the lane and in sight of the mill,
   Is the smithy; I pass it to-day, in a dream
Of the days whose red blood in my bosom is warm
   While the real alone as the vanish'd I deem:
For the years they may crumble to dust in the heart,
But the roses will bloom though the gravestones
    depart.

In the loneliest evenings of long ago,
   The smithy was dear in the darkness to me,
When the clouds were all heaping the world with
    their snow,
   And the wind shiver'd over dead leaves on the
    tree;
Through the snow-shower it seemed to be bursting
    aflame:
How the sparks in the dark from the chimney
    came!

THE DESERTED SMITHY.

It was dear in the past—and still it is dear,
   In the memory old of the vanishing time,
When the binging and banging, and clinging and
     clanging,
   In the heart of my boyhood, were music and
     rhyme;
When the bellows groan'd to the furnace-glow,
And the lights thro' the chinks danced out in the
     snow.

The irons within on the anvils were ringing:
   There were glowing arms in the bursting gleam;
And shadows were glowering away in the gloaming,
   That, suddenly bounding to giants, would seem
Now out of the open doorways to spring,
Now up in the rafters vanishing.

The smith I remember: oh, many a smile
   Has played on his lips with me, and kind
Were the words that would lighten the gloom of his
     face—
   His face, at the memory, gleams in my mind!—
With a heart that could beat in the heart of a
     boy,
A heart for his sorrow, a heart for his joy!

THE DESERTED SMITHY.

Adown from the farm of my father once more
  (That so long has forgotten us up on the hill)—
With the wings in my blood to the bound of the
    steed,
  That passes the breezes so merry and shrill—
I seem to be flying ; but, suddenly,
In the Past, alone, is my memory !

In a dream !—in a dream !   But I pass it to-day :
  No longer the furnace is bursting with flame ;
No longer the music comes out of the door,
  That, long ago, to the schoolboy came :
The winds whisper low thro' the window and door,
The chimney is part of the dust of the floor.

Phœbe Morris ! sweet Phœbe ! the sweetest of girls
  That brighten'd old dreams with a beautiful face !—
It may be she smiled from her father's lips,
  And blossom'd her smile in the dusky place !
Ah, she smiles, to-day, in my boyhood for me,
With her lips that are kissing—a memory !

THE FIRST TRYST.

She pulls a rose from her rose-tree,
　Kissing its soul to him—
Far over years, far over dreams
　And tides of chances dim.

He plucks from his heart a poem ;
　A flower-sweet messenger,
Far over years, far over dreams,
　Flutters its soul to her.

These are the world-old lovers,
　Clasped in one twilight's gleam :
Yet he is but a dream to her,
　And she a poet's dream.

LEAVES AT MY WINDOW.

I WATCH the leaves that flutter in the wind,
Bathing my eyes with coolness and my heart
Filling with springs of grateful sense anew,
Before my window—in the sun and rain.
And now the wind is gone and now the rain,
And all a motionless moment breathe, and now
Playful the wind comes back—again the shower,
Again the sunshine!   Like a golden swarm
Of butterflies the leaves are fluttering,
The leaves are dancing, singing—all alive
(For Fancy gives her breath to every leaf)
For the blithe moment.   Beautiful to me,
Of all inanimate things most beautiful,
And dear as flowers their kindred, are the leaves
In all their summer life ; and, when a child,
I loved to lie through sunny afternoons
With half-shut eyes (familiar eyes with things
Long unfamiliar, knowing Fairyland
And all the unhidden mysteries of the Earth)
Using my kinship in those earlier days
With Nature and the humbler people, dear

To her green life, in every shade and sun.
The leaves had myriad voices, and their joy
One with the birds, that sang among them seem'd :
And, oftentimes, I lay in breezy shade
Till, creeping with the loving stealth he takes
In healthy temperaments, the blessèd Sleep
(Thrice blessèd and thrice-blessing now, because
Of sleepless things that will not give us rest)
Came with his weird processions—dreams that
　　　　wore
All happy masks—blithe fairies numberless,
Forever passing, never more to pass,
The Spirits of the Leaves.　Awaking then,
Behold the sun was swimming in my face
Through mists of his creations, swarming gold,
And all the leaves in sultry languor lay
Above me, for I waken'd when they dropp'd
Asleep, unmoving.　Now, when Time has ceased
His holiday, and I am prison'd close
In his harsh service, master'd by his Hours,
The leaves have not forgotten me : behold,
They play with me like children who, awake,
Find one most dear asleep and waken him
To their own gladness from his sultry dream ;
But nothing sweeter do they give to me

6　　　　　　61

LEAVES AT MY WINDOW.

Than thoughts of one who, far away, perchance
Watches like me the leaves and thinks of me
While o'er her window, sunnily, the shower
Touches all boughs to music, and the rose
Beneath swings lovingly toward the pane,
And She, whom Nature gave the freshest sense
For all her delicate life, rejoices in
The joy of birds that use the sun to sing
With breasts o'er-full of music.   "Little Birds,"
She sings, "Sing to my little Bird below!"
And with her child-like fancy, half-belief,
She hears them sing and makes-believe they obey,
And the child, wakening, listens motionless.

FROST ON THE PANES.

BEFORE my window standing
  I see the dream-like glow
Of Frost against the dawning :
  Old fancies come and go.

A little child is gazing,
  With wonder-lighted eyes,
Before the white enchantment
  That veils the morning skies.

His mother steals beside him :
  The marvellous picture gleams—
The Fairy, Frost, has painted
  His Fairy world of dreams !

Weird woodlands shine enchanted
  With crystal boughs so bright,
Where ghouls alone have wander'd ;
  Strange castles haunt the night.

FROST ON THE PANES.

Lo, while the child is gazing,
   The white enchantment 's fled,
And I, alone, awaken,
   And Fairyland is dead !

I look out through the window :
   The market roars and beats,
With myriad wheels and footsteps
   The crowded morning streets.

Tears stand upon the window,
   For the frost-work's fragile gleam,
And on my cheek are tear-drops,
   Old relics of my dream.

Tears shine upon the window,
   Where the frost-work flash'd before
Ah, in Time's Eastern windows
   Are frosted panes no more !

THE UNHEARD BELL.

SOMEWHERE a Bell speaks, deep and slow,
The ancient monotone of woe :
A child within a garden bright,
The Paradise of morning light,
Hears fountain-laughter, songs of birds,
And teaches Echo mirthful words.

Somewhere a Bell speaks, deep and slow,
The ancient monotone of woe :
A youth in an enchanted grove
Hears maidens singing lays of love ;
Restless he seeks them all the day,
To crown the loveliest Queen of May.

Somewhere a Bell speaks, deep and slow,
The ancient monotone of woe :
A man, in streets of dust and heat,
Hears the wide sound of busy feet,
The great world's moving, ceaselessly ;
And dusk sails whiten far at sea.

THE UNHEARD BELL.

Somewhere a Bell speaks, deep and slow,
The ancient monotone of woe :
An old man—dead to wingéd song,
To maiden voice, or moving throng—
Hears not within his hearse the knell,
The black procession of the Bell.

THE GOLDEN HAND.

Lo, from the city's heat and dust
A Golden Hand forever thrust,
Uplifting from a spire on high
A shining finger in the sky!

I see it when the morning brings
Fresh tides of life to living things,
And the great world awakes : behold,
That lifted Hand in morning gold!

I see it when the noontide beats
Pulses of fire in busy streets ;
The dust flies in the flaming air :
Above, that quiet Hand is there.

I see it when the twilight clings
To the dark earth with hovering wings :
Flashing with the last fluttering ray,
That Golden Hand remembers day.

67

THE GOLDEN HAND.

The midnight comes—the holy hour;
The city like a giant flower
Sleeps full of dew : that Hand, in light
Of moon and stars, how weirdly bright !

Below, in many a noisy street
Are toiling hands and striving feet;
The weakest rise, the strongest fall :
That equal Hand is over all.

Below, in courts to guard the land,
Gold buys the tongue and binds the hand
Stealing in God's great scales the gold,
That awful Hand, above, behold !

Below, the Sabbaths walk serene
With the great dust of Days between;
Preachers within their pulpits stand :
See, over all, that heavenly Hand !

But the hot dust, in crowded air
Below, arises never there :
O speech of one who cannot speak !
O Sabbath-witness of the Week !

MARIAN'S FIRST HALF-YEAR.

Maiden Marian, born in May,
When the earth with flowers was gay,
And the Hours by day and night
Wore the jewels of delight:
Half-a-year has vanish'd by
Like a wondrous pageantry—
Mother May with fairy flowers,
June with dancing leaf-crown'd Hours,
July red with harvest-rust,
Swarthy August white with dust,
Mild September clothed in gold,
Wise October, hermit old—
And the world, so new and strange,
Circled you in olden change,
Since the miracle-morn of birth
Made your May-day on the earth.
Half-a-year, sweet child, has brought
To your eyes the soul of thought;
To your lips, with cries so dumb,
Baby-syllables have come,

MARIAN'S FIRST HALF-YEAR.

Dreams of fairy language known
To your mother's heart alone—
Anté-Hebrew words complete
(To old Noah obsolete) ;
You have learn'd expressions strange,
Miracles of facial change,
Winning gestures, supplications,
Stamp'd entreaties, exhortations—
Oratory eloquent
Where no more is said than meant ;
You have lived philosophies
Older far than Socrates—
Holiest life you've understood
Better than oldest wise and good :
Such as erst in Eden's light
Shunn'd not God's nor angels' sight ;
You have caught with subtler eyes
Close Pythagorean ties
In the bird and in the tree,
And in every thing you see ;
You have found and practise well
(Moulding life of principle)
Epicurean doctrines old
Of the Hour's fruit of gold :
Lifted, Moses-like, you stand,
Looking, where the Promised Land

MARIAN'S FIRST HALF-YEAR.

Dazzles far away your sight—
Milk-and-honey's your delight!
   Maiden Marian, born in May
Half-a-year has pass'd away;
Half-a-year of cannon-pealing,
('Twas your era of good feeling,)
You have scarce heard dreader sound
Than those privateers around,
Buzzing flies, a busy brood,
Lovers of sweet babyhood—
Than the hum of lullaby
Rock'd to dreamland tenderly;
Half-a-year of dreadest sights
Through bright days and fairy nights,
You have seen no dreader thing
Than the marvel of a wing,
Than the leaves whose shadows warm
Play'd in many a phantom swarm
On the floor, the table under,
Lighting your small face with wonder!
   Maiden Marian, born in May,
Half-a-year has pass'd away:
'Tis a dark November day;
Lifted by our window, lo!
Washington is whirl'd in snow!
But, within, the fluttering flame

MARIAN'S FIRST HALF-YEAR.

Keeps you summer-warm the same,
And your mother (while I write),
Crimson'd by the ember light,
Murmurs sweeter things to you
Than I'd write a half-year through :
Baby-lyrics, lost to art,
Found within a mother's heart.
  Maiden Marian, born in May,
I'll not question Time to-day
For the mysteries of your morrows,
Girlhood's joys or woman's sorrows,
But (while—side by side, alone—
We recall your summer flown,
And, with eyes that cannot look,
Hold his claspéd Mystery-Book)
I will trust when May is here
He shall measure you a year,
With another half-year sweet
Make the ring of light complete :
We will date our New-Years thence,
Full of summer songs and sense—
All the years begun that day
Shall be born and die in May !

NOVEMBER 7, 1862.

CHARITY AT HOME.

Two children stand, with dimpled cheek and chin,
  Pressing their loving foreheads to the pane
  To see the forest black in twilight rain,
But only see their happy walls within,
  Winking in firelight, wavering rosy-warm,
  While rush without, roaring, the wings of storm.

So, often, we who in charm'd circles stand,
  Where the good Fairy, Fortune, smiling brings
  God's transient gifts with ever-gracious wings,
Behold the world in her closed Fairyland:
  For, warm within, from our sweet rooms we gaze
  Into the dark, and see—our Fireside-blaze!

7   78

MOONRISE.

'Tis midnight and the city lies
With dreaming heart and closéd eyes:
The giant's folded hands at rest,
Like Prayer asleep, are on his breast.

From windows hush'd, I see alone
The tide-worn streets so silent grown:
The dusty footprints of the day
Are bless'd with dew and steal away.

Oh, scarce a pulse of sound!   Afar,
Flashes upon a spire a star—
Lo, in the East a dusky light:
Ghost-like the moon moves through the night.

Unveiling slow, a face of blood
She lifts into the solitude!
The city sleeps; above, behold
The moonrise kiss a cross of gold!

MOONRISE.

Golden in air that cross : at rest
Below the city's sleeping breast ;
And on the cross, moon-brighten'd, see !
Christ, dying, smiles down lovingly !

75

NEW GRASS.

ALONG the sultry city street,
Faint subtile breaths of fragrance meet
      Me, wandering unaware
(In April warmth, while yet the sun
For Spring no constant place has won)
      By many a vacant square.

Whoever reads these lines has felt
That breath whose long-lost perfumes melt
      The spirit——newly found
While the sweet, banished families
Of earth's forgotten sympathies
      Rise from the sweating ground.

It is the subtile breath of grass;
And as I pause, or lingering pass,
      With half-shut eyes, behold!
Bright from old baptisms of dew
Fresh meadows burst upon my view,
      And new becomes the old!

NEW GRASS.

Old longings (Pleasure kissing Pain),
Old visions visit me again—
      Life's quiet deeps are stirr'd :
The fountain-heads of memory flow
Through channels dry so long ago,
      With music long unheard.

I think of pastures, evermore
Greener than any hour before,
      Where cattle wander slow,
Large-uddered in the sun, or chew
The cud content in shadows new,
      Or, shadows, homeward low.

I dream of prairies dear to me :
Afar in town I seem to see
      Their widening miles arise,
Where, like the butterfly anear,
Far off in sunny mist the deer,
      That seems no larger, flies.

Thy rural lanes, Ohio, come
Back to me, grateful with the hum
      Of every thing that stirs :
Dear places, sadden'd by the years,
Lost to my sight send sudden tears,
      Their secret messengers.

NEW GRASS.

I think of paths a-swarm with wings
Of bird and bee—all lovely things
      From sun or sunny clod ;
Of play-grounds where the children play,
And fear not Time will come to-day,
      And feel the warming sod.

New grass : it grows by cottage doors,
In orchards hush'd with bloom, by shores
      Of streams that flow as green,
On hill-slopes white with tents or sheep,
And where the sacred mosses keep
      The holy dead unseen.

It grows o'er distant graves I know—
Sweet grass ! above them greener grow,
      And guard them tenderly !
My brother's, not three summers green ;
My sister's—new-made, only seen
      Through far-off tears by me !

It grows on battle-fields—alas !
Old battle-fields are lost in grass ;
      New battles wait the new :
Hark, is it the living warmth I hear ?
The cannon far or bee anear ?
      The bee and cannon too !

WASHINGTON, April, 1863.

FIRE BEFORE SEED.*

How bright to-night lies all the Vale,
   Where Autumn scatter'd harvest gold
And, far off, humm'd the rumbling flail
   When dark autumnal noons were cold!

The fields put on a mask of fire,
   Forever changing, in the dark;
Lo, yonder upland village spire
   Flashes in air a crimson spark!

I see the farm-house roofs arise,
   Among their guardian elms asleep:
Redly the flame each window dyes,
   Through vines that chill and leafless creep.

* It is customary in some portions of the West to rake the
last year's stubble of corn into windrows and burn it preparatory
to breaking the ground in Spring for a new planting. This burn-
ing is generally done after nightfall: its effect on the landscape
these lines were intended to describe.

FIRE BEFORE SEED.

Along the lonely lane, that goes
    Darkening beyond the dusky hill,
Amid the light the cattle doze
    And sings the 'waken'd April rill.

The mill by rocks is shadow'd o'er,
    But, overhead, the shimmering trees
Stand sentinels of the rocky shore
    And bud with fire against the breeze !

Afar the restless ripple shakes
    Arrows of splendor through the wood,
Then all its noisy water breaks
    Away in glimmering solitude.

Gaze down into the bottoms near,
    Where all the darkness broadly warms
The priests who guard the fires appear
    Gigantic shadows, pigmy forms !

The enchanted Spring shall here awake
    With harvest hope among her flowers ;
And nights of holy dew shall make
    The morning smile for toiling hours.

FIRE BEFORE SEED.

Behold the Sower's sacrifice
   Upon the altars of the Spring !—
O dead Past, into flame arise :
   New seed into the earth we fling !

THE BOOK OF GOLD.

I.

If I could write a Book made sweet with thee,
And therefore sweet with all that may be sweet,
With lingering music never more complete
Should turn its golden pages : each should be
Like whispering voices, beckoning hands, and he
Who read should follow, while his heart would
      beat
For some new miracle, with most eager feet
Through loving labyrinths of mystery.
Temple and lighted home of Love should seem
The Book wherein my love remember'd thine :
There holiest visions evermore should gleam,
Vanishing wings, with wandering souls of sound
And breaths of incense from an inmost shrine
Sought nearer evermore and never found.

II.

Vague wishes, in my bosom, never cold
Brought these vague words to me one Summer
      night,
Longing to prison in crystal the sweet light

THE BOOK OF GOLD.

My soul had breathed and write a Book of Gold
To keep my love within the radiant fold
Of Love's true heraldry in histories bright;
And Love, the only poet, whisper'd " Write,"
When I began with impulse overbold
Which had dumb lips—then, turning, spake to
     Love :
" Sweet Master, how shall I, unskilful, know
To speak of thee and thine, all things above ?"
" I still shall hold thy hand and guide thy heart;
Let what is mine be thine," he answer'd low,
" And what is artful Love's thy loving Art."

MY NIGHTMARE.

ALL day my nightmare in my thought I keep :
  Spell-bound, it seem'd, by some magician's
    charm,
  A giant slumber'd on my slothful arm—
His great, slow breathings jarr'd the land of sleep,
(Like far-off thunder, rumbling low and deep,)
  Lifting his brawny bosom bronzed and warm—
  When lo ! a voice shook me with stern alarm :
" Who art thou here that dost not sow nor reap ?
  Behold the Sleeping Servant of thy Day—
Arouse him to thy deed : if thou but break
  His slumberous spell, awake he will obey."
I lifted up my voice and cried " Awake !"
And I awoke !—my arm, unnerved, lay dead,
A useless thing beneath my sleeping head !

MY BIRTHDAY, 1863.

TO A POET: ON HIS MARRIAGE.

"THE Artist with his Art alone should wed,"
  They say, the worldly wise, "who runs may
    read;"
  And I would grant it holy truth indeed,
Did Art want men in whom the man was dead—
Pale priesthood. But with fullest life, instead,
  She ordains her truer worshippers: her need
  Is men who live as well as dream their deed;
She loves to see her lovers sweat for bread.
My friend, I know you not as one who bear,
  Dream-like, upon your soul the ideal sphere
And kick the real world beneath your feet:
I see you, brave young Atlas, lift in air
  The loving load of manhood, without fear.
Both worlds be one to you, a world complete!

II.

If you should ask me what your life should seem,
  Built by the great, slow mason, Time, for you,
  (My wishes being master-builders, too,)
I'd say a grand cathedral, with the stream

TO A POET: ON HIS MARRIAGE.

Of wondrous light through windows all a-gleam
   With heavenliest shapes and sacred histories
      true
   Of truest lives that e'er immortal grew
From low mortality's divinest dream.
Above, uplifted on some chaunt divine,
   An angel choir should cluster, dumb in stone;
Below, and rapt in the religious air,
Most saintly brows should with a halo shine:
   And, amid marble multitudes alone,
Lo! one sweet woman's face the holiest there!

A SABBATH IN JULY.

A YEAR ago to-day, the Sabbath hours
 Were sweet to us, wandering together, here
 In these green woods. The skies were soft and
  clear,
And the sun wrought his miracles in flowers.
Sweet was the Sabbath stillness of these bowers;
 The birds sang in the tender atmosphere,
 And God's own voice seem'd whispering low and
  near
To His hush'd children in those hearts of ours.
Lo! scarcely mingling with the real day,
 Far thunders beat in the heart of solitude,
Echoes of Hell to Heaven's divine repose:
 For, while we breathed the breathless Sabbath
  wood,
The cannon's awful monotone arose
 Where the dread Sabbath-breaking Preacher
  stood!

July 21, 1862.

A BUST IN CLAY.*

S. P. C.

A NOBLE soul is breathing from the clay,
  Created, Sculptor, with a soul by thee ;
  A noble soul a noble man's must be :
One of a few, he knelt not to the Day
Nor petty stampings of the applausive Hour,
  But, in the dark of her uprising light,
  Upheld in word and served in deed the Right,
Nor sued the million-headed mob for power.
O beautiful ! on the calm lips, content,
Breathes the high presence of a life well spent ;
Such brows the centuries love ! No marble needs
His soul that carves itself in marble deeds·:
Oh, be it long—Ohio's prayer my own—
Ere clay or marble keeps that soul, alone !

January, 1859.

* By T. D. JONES, Sculptor, Cincinnati, Ohio.

SONNET—IN 1862.

STERN be the Pilot in the dreadful hour
   When a great nation, like a ship at sea
   With the wroth breakers whitening at her lee,
Feels her last shudder if her Helmsman cower;
A godlike manhood be his mighty dower!
   Such and so gifted, Lincoln, may'st thou be
   With thy high wisdom's low simplicity
And awful tenderness of voted power:
From our hot records then thy name shall stand
   On Time's calm ledger out of passionate days—
With the pure debt of gratitude begun
   And only paid in never-ending praise—
One of the many of a mighty Land
Made by God's providence the Anointed One.

TO R. C. S.

DEAR General, in the Age of Chivalry—
   That Golden Age of Manhood, whose lost seed
   Blossom'd in you—true men of loyal breed
Bow'd under kingly swords, on bended knee,
And rose with Knighthood holy, sworn to be
   Champions of Right and guardians at her need,
   Their life the errand of some noble deed
Halo'd by History, crown'd by Poesy.
But Nature, first Knight-maker then as now,
   (For Kings were but her servants and are still,)
Put her great seal of Knighthood on your brow,
   And we behold you sacred to her will,
Knowing why on your thigh the sword is seen
And on your hair the civic wreath is green.

Benjamin M. Piatt.

Ob. April 20, 1863—Æt. 84.

Near his loved home, among familiar flowers,
(Whose memories mingle fragrant breath with ours,)
Sleeps a gray father of the mighty West.
His hands had Nature's plea for folded rest :
For, through long years and manhood's noble strife,
Whiten'd his head above his golden life.
He pass'd as one who from his harvest goes,
Attended by the sun, to his repose—
Gracious and good.   Behold his simple fame :
He lies asleep beneath his honor'd name.

THE BIRTHDAYS.

O MORNING, sweet and bright and clear!
　　Anew the earth seems blossoming :
In Summer's swarthy heart I hear
　　The fountain-heads of Spring.

It is your birthday, dearest one—
　　Far-off from you this summer day,
I think of many another sun
　　That August took from May.

When—for your honor—sweet and bright,
　　The month of dust and dead perfume
Remember'd May's delicious light,
　　Her gentle breath and bloom.

I dream of many a birthday blithe,
　　Baptizing earth with loving dew,
When Time the reaper hid his scythe
　　And gather'd flowers for you.

92

THE BIRTHDAYS.

Lo, first I see the morning, love,
   That on your mother's tender breast,
A wingless bird from Heaven above,
   You found your earthly nest.

Your childhood's birthdays come and go,
   Stealing from shining day to day
A lovely child with whom, I know,
   The fairies loved to play.

Your grand old kinsman, Boone, I guess—
   Ulysses of the Indian wild—
Enjoy'd no dearer loneliness
   Than you a wandering child.

Shy as the butterfly you went
   On visits to your baby flowers,
Among the lonely birds content
   To pass unlonely hours.

Nature, I deem, those birthdays caught
   You to her breast in solitude :
Her loveliest picture-books she brought
   And read you in the wood.

THE BIRTHDAYS.

All lovely things she gave your love :
   The humble flowers, the stars on high,
The lightning's awful wing above,
   The tremulous butterfly.

My fancy, love-created, goes
   Lightly from passing year to year :
My little fairy maiden grows
   To tender girlhood dear.

A dreaming girl, as shy as dew
   In dells of Fairyland apart,
Within your soul a lily grew—
   A rose within your heart.

I follow on your changeful way,
   Lift all the burdens from your hours,
Make you my constant queen of May
   And wreathe your birthday flowers.

My fancy follows : ah, perchance,
   I, Fairy Prince of fable true,
Found you asleep in fated trance
   And kiss'd you ere you knew !

THE BIRTHDAYS.

They come, they vanish—swift or slow—
 Oh, long unmask'd, those maskéd years:
At last the birthdays that I know
 I see, with smiles and tears.

Your birthdays which are mine draw nigh:
 Lo, yours and mine are join'd in one!—
Mine with the blue-bird's prophecy,
 Yours with the August sun!

And, look, another joins the two:
 The First of March, the August day
Mingle their tender light and dew
 With Marian's in May!

TO GRACE AT CHRISTMAS.

WITH AN EASTERN FAIRY-BOOK.

Sweet Fairyland! at Christmas, lo!
    Thy sunken splendors shine
To those who, Westward, farther go
    Out of the East divine——
Dear wonder-world by childhood won,
Lost Miracle of the Morning sun!

A blind man prison'd in the light,
    Still, as a blinded man, I look
At the old shapes of vanish'd sight
    In Memory's Marvel-Book
I turn the pages, leaf by leaf,
And Fancy makes-believe belief!

But now at charmed words, alas!
    The treasure-doors have Treasury locks
Aladdin's lamp (or gold or brass?)
    I rub: the Genius knocks!——
This coal-oil lamp was just in place:
" Come in"——a Genius? No, a Grace!

TO GRACE AT CHRISTMAS.

Sweet little maiden, to your sight
   Fairies and Fairy-worlds may rise;
The East to you shows joyous light
   Where in his cradle lies
God's Gentle Child—this lovely morn
I saw him dead and crown'd with thorn!

A dreamer's fancy—never mind ;
   You'd have a Fairy-Book, you said :
A gift of sunshine gives the blind—
   When the sweet dreams are dead,
I pray that from your eyes and heart
Faith, the True Fairy, 'll ne'er depart!

DECEMBER 25, 1862.

MOTHS.

At morn I walk in sunshine warm and tender;
  My eyes look into Fairyland for hours:
The butterflies with Eastern lust and splendor
  Grow wingéd counterparts to wingless flowers.

At noon I dream in meadows sweet and sunny;
  My heart with summer songs and perfume glows:
The bees on sunburnt voyages for honey
  Reach their Hesperides in every rose.

At eve I write by restless lamplight sitting;
  My soul is full of shadowy, subtile things:
The ghostly moths around my lamp are flitting,
  Guests of the light that, coming, lose their wings.

My poems, butterflies at morning gleaming,
  And bees at noon, are but vague moths at night:
Look, the flame beckons—from the darkness stream
      ing,
  Wingless they drop at thresholds of the light!

I I .

𝔄 . 𝔅 . 𝔜 .

TO THE WORLD.

Sweet World, if you will hear me now:
  I may not own a sounding Lyre
And wear my name upon my brow
  Like some great jewel full of fire.

But let me, singing, sit apart,
  In tender quiet with a few,
And keep my fame upon my heart,
  A little blush-rose wet with dew.

HEARING THE BATTLE.—July 21, 1861.

One day in the dreamy summer,
  On the Sabbath hills, from afar
We heard the solemn echoes
  Of the first fierce words of war.

Ah, tell me, thou veiléd Watcher
  Of the storm and the calm to come,
How long by the sun or shadow
  Till these noises again are dumb.

And soon in a hush and glimmer
  We thought of the dark, strange fight,
Whose close in a ghastly quiet
  Lay dim in the beautiful night.

Then we talk'd of coldness and pallor,
  And of things with blinded eyes
That stared at the golden stillness
  Of the moon in those lighted skies ;

HEARING THE BATTLE.

And of souls, at morning wrestling
    In the dust with passion and moan,
So far away at evening
    In the silence of worlds unknown.

But a delicate wind beside us
    Was rustling the dusky hours,
As it gather'd the dewy odors
    Of the snowy jessamine-flowers.

And I gave you a spray of the blossoms,
    And said : " I shall never know
How the hearts in the land are breaking,
    My dearest, unless you go."

MY GHOST.

Yes, Katie, I think you are very sweet,
    Now that the tangles are out of your hair,
And you sing as well as the birds you meet,
    That are playing, like you, in the blossoms there.
But now you are coming to kiss me, you say:
    Well, what is it for?   Shall I tie your shoe,
Or loop your sleeve in a prettier way?
    "Do I know about ghosts?"   Indeed I do.

"Have I seen one?"   Yes: last evening, you
        know,
    We were taking a walk that you had to miss,
(I think you were naughty and cried to go,
    But, surely, you'll stay at home after this!)
And, away in the twilight lonesomely
    ("What is the twilight?"   It's—getting late!)
I was thinking of things that were sad to me—
    There, hush! you know nothing about them,
        Kate.

105

MY GHOST.

Well, we had to go through the rocky lane,
    Close to that bridge where the water roars,
By a still, red house, where the dark and rain
    Go in when they will at the open doors;
And the moon, that had just waked up, look'd through
    The broken old windows and seem'd afraid,
And the wild bats flew and the thistles grew
    Where once in the roses the children play'd.

Just across the road by the cherry-trees
    Some fallen white stones had been lying so long,
Half hid in the grass, and under these
    There were people dead. I could hear the song
Of a very sleepy dove, as I pass'd
    The graveyard near, and the cricket that cried;
And I look'd (ah! the Ghost is coming at last!)
    And something was walking at my side.

It seem'd to be wrapp'd in a great dark shawl,
    (For the night was a little cold, you know;)
It would not speak. It was black and tall;
    And it walk'd so proudly and very slow.
Then it mock'd me—every thing I could do:
    Now it caught at the lightning-flies like me;
Now it stopp'd where the elder-blossoms grew;
    Now it tore the thorns from an old dead tree.

MY GHOST.

Still it follow'd me under the yellow moon,
   Looking back to the graveyard now and then,
Where the winds were playing the night a tune—
   But, Kate, a Ghost does n't care for *men*,
And your papa *couldn't* have done it harm!
   Ah, dark-eyed darling, what is it you see?
There, you needn't hide in your dimpled arm—
   It was only my Shadow that walk'd with me!

TO MARIAN ASLEEP.

THE full moon glimmers still and white,
   Where yonder shadowy clouds unfold;
The stars, like children of the Night,
   Lie with their little heads of gold
On her dark lap: nor less divine,
And brighter, seems your own on mine.

My darling, with your snowy sleep
   Folded around your dimpled form,
Your little breathings calm and deep,
   Your mother's arms and heart are warm
You wear as lilies in your breast
The dreams that blossom from your rest.

Ah, must your clear eyes see ere long
   The mist and wreck on sea and land,
And that old haunter of all song,
   The mirage hiding in the sand?
And will the dead leaves in the frost
Tell you of song and summer lost?

And shall you hear the ghastly tales
   From the slow, solemn lips of Time—
Of Wrong that wins, of Right that fails,
   Of trampled Want and gorgeous Crime,
Of Splendor's glare in lighted rooms
And Famine's moan in outer glooms ?

Of armies in their red eclipse
   That mingle on the smoking plain ;
Of storms that dash our mighty ships
   With silks and spices through the main
Of what it costs to climb or fall—
Of Death's great Shadow ending all ?

But, baby Marian, do I string
   The dark with darker rhymes for you,
Forgetting that you came in Spring,
   The child of sun and bloom and dew,
And that I kiss'd, still fresh to-day,
The rosiest bud of last year's May ?

Forgive me, pretty one : I know,
   Whatever sufferings onward lie,
Christ wore his crown of thorns below
   To gain his crown of light on high ;
And when the lamp's frail flame is gone,
Look up : the stars will still shine on.

TO MARIAN ASLEEP.

Yet flowers that blossom from the ground
   Are not all asphodels, my sweet:
Such rare, pure love as I have found
   Grows in the present at our feet:
I err'd to tell you of the grave—
Heaven is the end, and God can save.

GASLIGHT AND STARLIGHT.

THOSE flowers of flame that blossom at night
  From the dust of the city, along the street,
And wreathe rich rooms with their leaves of light,
  Were dropping their tremulous bloom at my feet.

And the men whose names by the crowd are known
  And the women uplifted to share their place—
Some of them bright with their jewels alone,
  Some of them brighter with beauty and grace—

Were around me under the flashing rays,
  All seeming, I thought as I saw them there,
To ask the throng, in their pleased, mute ways,
  For its bow, or its smile, or at least its stare.

But, faint with the odors that floated about,
  And tired of the glory the few can win,
I turned to the window—the darkness without
  Struck heavily on the glitter within,

GASLIGHT AND STARLIGHT.

Still the glare behind me haunted my brain,
   And I thought : " They are blest who are shining
      so ; "
But a voice replied : " You are blinded and vain—
   Such triumph when highest is often low.

" For some," it said, with a slow, sad laugh—
   " Who wear so proudly their little names,
Have leant on the People, as on a staff
   To help them up to their selfish fames.

" And others yet—it is hard to know—
   Have crawl'd through the dust to their sunny hour,
To crawl the same in its warmth and glow
   And hiss the snake in the colors of Power.

" Yet it is comfort to feel, through the whole,
   They only look great, in God's calm eyes,
Who lean on the still, grand strength of the soul
   And climb toward the pure, high light of the skies."

112

A DREAM'S AWAKENING.

Shut in a close and dreary sleep,
  Lonely and frightened and oppress'd
I felt a dreadful serpent creep,
  Writhing and crushing, o'er my breast.

I woke and knew my child's sweet arm,
  As soft and pure as flakes of snow,
Beneath my dream's dark, hateful charm,
  Had been the thing that tortured so.

And, in the morning's dew and light
  I seem'd to hear an angel say,
" The Pain that stings in Time's low night
  May prove God's Love in higher day."

TO A DEAD BIRD.

Bird of the forest, beautiful and dead!
　While in the twilight here I gaze on thee,
Strange fancies, of the wild life that has fled,
　Dimly and sadly gather over me,
Until, above thy calm and silent sleep,
I can but bow my aching head and weep.

Alas, that when the spring-time's here to wake
　The flowers and music of thy woodland halls,
Thou whose glad voice so sweet a strain could make
　In concert with the winds and water-falls,
In cold and hushed oblivion shouldst lie—
While things that suffer ask, in vain, to die!

But, wast thou purely blest?　Ah, who can tell
　But birds may have their sorrows?　It may be
That boundless love in thy small breast did dwell
　For some bright, wingéd thing—that flew from
　　　thee
And left his scorn to pierce thy bleeding heart,
Till Death, in pity, drew away its dart!

114

TO A DEAD BIRD.

Or thine, perchance, has been a perfect love,
  (If any love can be without a sting !)
And thy lone mate may come to mourn above
  Thy blighted beauty, with a drooping wing,
Till, like all lonely mates, he seeks relief,
In some new rapture, for his transient grief !

Or thou mayst have been of a royal race !
  And radiant throngs of minstrel-things to-day,
Even in thy airy realm's remotest place,
  May mourn, or joy, that thou hast pass'd away !
For gold and purple glitter on thy breast,
And thou art laid right regally to rest.

Was thy death tranquil ?   Or, amid the glare
  Of Heaven's fierce fire-arms was thy being sped ?
Or did some wing'd assassin of the air,
  For hate, or envy, meet and strike thee dead ?
Was life still blushing with youth's rosy glow,
Or, worn and wearied, wast thou glad to go ?

And was thy all of joy, or grief, on earth ?
  Or art thou gone to try thy wing anew
Where glorious roses have their perfumed birth,
  And woods are ever green, skies ever blue,
And breezy music gushes rich and warm,
With not a sigh, or whisper of the storm ?

TO A DEAD BIRD.

Fit mausoleum is this hollow tree,
   With faded leaves to pillow thy bright head
And, if such rest is all that's left for thee,
   Methinks it is enough, sweet singer dead!
For winds will sing and buds will burst above,
And I'll believe they left thee here in love!

A DISENCHANTMENT.

And thou wast but a breathing May
   Embodied by delicious dreams,
And drifted o'er my wandering way
   On fancy's swift and shining streams.
Thine eyes were only violets,
   Thy lips but buds of crimson bloom,
Thy hair, coiled sunshine—vain regrets!
   Thy soul, a brief perfume.

And when the time of mists and chills
   Fell where the sweet wild roses grew,
And took them from the shadowy hills,
   It took my lovely vision too;
And when I came again to find
   The charm which used to fill the air,
A sorrow struck me mute and blind—
   Thou wast not anywhere!

Yet something met me in thy place,
   Something, they said, with looks like thine,
With tresses full of golden grace
   And lips flush'd red with beauty's wine;

With voice of silvery swells and falls
  And dreamy eyes still sweetly blue—
But, then, the reptile's nature crawls
  Beneath the rainbow's hue.

Woman, all things below, above,
  Look pale and drear and glimmering now,
For I have loved thee with a love
  Whose passionate deeps such things as thou
May never sound. And, with a moan,
  The chill'd tide of that love has rolled
Above my heart, and made it stone,
  And oh, so cold, so cold!

I saw thee by a magic lamp
  Whose warm and gorgeous blaze is gone,
And o'er me shivers, gray and damp,
  The dimness of the real's dawn.
Oh, I am like to one who stands
  Where late a vision smiled in air,
And murmurs, with outstretching hands,
  " Where is my Angel—where ?"

A CHAIN FROM VENICE.

SHE stretches dimpled arms of snow;
    A glad smile lights her baby eyes:
My little beauty, would you know
    The story of your shining prize?

It is a poet's golden thought
    Of you, that glitters like your hair,
Of rich Venetian sunlight wrought
    Far in the South's enchanted air.

Ah, if you stay from Heaven to learn
    The years before you lying dim,
You'll think, my darling, in return,
    A thought as beautiful of him.

IN THE GRAVEYARD.

THE sweetness dropp'd from the cherry-blooms
 Over the sleep that is never stirr'd,
And the twilight droop'd on her purple plumes,
 And flutter'd and moan'd, like a dying bird,
Till I hid my face in the scented glooms.

The grasses were damp where the thorns had grown
 The bats flew close to the mouldering staves ;
Some wild, white buds, with a windy moan,
 Fell with their faces against the graves,
And the moss-veils hung on the broken stone.

Out of the dim and dusky sky
 A golden blossoming broke ere long,
And glitter'd and fell on the spring-woods nigh,
 Where a dove was hushing her sleepy song ;
And we were together, the dead and I.

" The heart above, with its breaking strings,
   Wails dissonant music, stormy or slow ;
But ah ! what a beautiful stillness clings,
   Sweet Death," I said, " to the hearts below,
That are touch'd with the calm of your pallid wings.

" But is memory still where the vanished go ?"
   Then I thought of a tender dream of the past,
That faded and fell in a passionate woe,
   Like a lotus-flower in a poison'd blast ;
And I stared in the shadow and said, " You know.

" Come out of your silence once more, and seem
   The thing that I loved in the years afar,
While the wild-bird flutters and sings in its dream,
   And the yellow bloom of the evening star
Drops, as of old, in the whispering stream."

You came, and I saw the tremulous breeze
   Blow the loose brown hair about your head ;
You came, thro' a murmur of melodies ;
   You came, for love can awaken the dead ;
You came, and stood by the cherry-trees.

IN THE GRAVEYARD.

You came, and your white hand was not cold,
  And your quiet eyes, they were not dim ;
And we watched the moon-rise dripping with gold,
  While the waters chanted a vesper hymn,
And your lip was flush'd with the tales it told.

I could see the wings of the sun's pet birds,
  I could hear the delicate sigh of the shells,
And the giant cry of the seas in your words ;
  Yet others had heard but the distant bells,
And seen but the glimmer of rocks and herds.

I whisper'd like one that is not awake :
  " Does sorrow die with our dying breath ?
Did it drop from your life like a wounded snake,
  When the dust of your beauty was touch'd with
    death ?
Oh, tell me, oh, tell me, for love's sweet sake.

" Say, is memory still, where the vanished go ?
  Say, Presence out of the spicy zones—
Let your sweet lip whisper the secret low,
  While I wait by the mosses and broken stones :
Ah, you hide in your silence, and yet you know."

A YEAR.—MDCCCLX.

My spirit saw a scene
Whose splendors were so terrible and bright
That the infinitude of mist between
The earth and sky scarce saved its eagle-sight
From being blasted.   In the middle night
He stood, the Guardian Angel of the Years:
His wings—that could extend their quenchless light
Across eternity, and rock the spheres
With their immortal strength—were folded now,
Like a still veil of glory, on his brow.

One fiery star and vast,
A gem to note the year, forever more
Burn'd in his ancient crown; and fierce and fast
Escaped the flame from out the one he wore,
Whose dimness vaguely settled on each shore
Along the seas of space; and, pale and lone,
But kingly with the solemn pride of yore,
Clinching the grandeur of a shadowy throne,
As if to hold his royalty from Death,
One lean'd beside him with an icy breath.

Nor earth, nor heaven will save
Us from the Doom which claim'd that mighty thing;
But, then, who fears or thinks upon the grave—
That narrow dark through which the free may spring
To the wide light beyond?   Who seeks to cling
With coward grasp to fetters and to strife?
Death is the only halcyon whose white wing
Can still the billows of a restless life.
Yet, were the present peace, the future woe,
New storms are better than a calm, we know.

He said, " My sceptre cast
Its shadows far as God's dominions lie;
Storms blew their thunder-trumpets as I pass'd,
And lightnings follow'd me about the sky.
I clasped th' unwilling worlds and heard them sigh
Against my breast with all their winds and waves;
Ay, as my victor chariot hurried by
Sun, star, and comet, like affrighted slaves,
Flung portions of their measured light below
Its silent wheels to make a triumph glow

" I passed yon radiant crowd
Of constellations, and there knelt beside
The Cross upon whose like a God has bow'd;
I met the mourning Pleiades, and cried

To their lost sister in th' unanswering tide
 Of night; I struck weird music from the Lyre,
And humbled old Orion's sullen pride,
 Who lean'd against his cimeter of fire,
And, with submissive reverence and mute,
Acknowledged my imperious salute.

   " Look, look—for all his deeds
Must pass before the sight of him who dies ;
 Mine crowd the infinite spaces—but man needs
Not to be told of those whose scenery lies
Beyond the bounds he knows, for his dim eyes
 See but the things I have around him wrought ;
He will not hear the dirge that soon must rise
 For me in all the myriad realms his thought
May visit, only by the hazy route
That glimmers round the reeling sails of Doubt.

   " The shadow of his world,
Like a dark canvas spread before me seems :
 There hides the hermit West, with cataracts whirl'd
Among the rocks, watching their foamy beams ;
There are the groves of myrrh, and diamond gleams,
 Where—fair as if it erewhile floated to
Its own warm poets, in their lotus dreams,
 As an ideal Aidenn, and there grew

A YEAR.

Into reality—the Orient lies
Close to the morn 'mid birds of Paradise.

      " There ice-mail'd warders keep
The gates of silence by the auroral rays
  Which fall above the cold-press'd North asleep,
Like a proud, pallid Queen, in the rich blaze
Of colored lamps, upon whose bosom weighs
  A dreary vision; and there, too, the sweet,
Sun-worshipp'd South in languid beauty stays,
  Like a sultana, caring but to meet
Her fiery lover 'mid her gorgeous bowers,
And, as his bride, be crown'd with orange flowers.

      " And, over all, there moves
The phantasm of my life.   With joy and dread
  I see it passing, and my memory proves
Its truth to nature.   Roses white and red,
Whose leaves into the winds have long been shed,
  And tremulous lily-bells, and jasmine blooms
Are there, as they had risen from the dead,
  So like their early selves their lost perfumes
Seem blown about them, and I hear the breeze
That used to kiss them sing old melodies.

      " Above, the changing sky
Shows wonder-pictures to my fading eyes:

A YEAR.

Now, the black armies of the clouds march by,
Now rainbows bloom, now golden moons arise.
Below, how varied too : now glitter lies
 On gorgeous jewels, bridal-flowers and mirth ;
Now mourners pass, and fill the air with sighs,
 To hide their coffins in the yawning earth ;
Now, with a pallid face and frenzied mind,
Cold, starving wretches ask if God is blind !

   " Now reels a nightmare throne
From the crush'd bosom of the Sicilies,
 The South's brief dream of blood wakes in the sun ;
Glad winds sing on the blue Italian seas,
And glad men bless me by their olive-trees ;
 Now, in the clouds above a younger land,
With awful eyes fix'd on its destinies,
 The frowning souls of its dead Glorious stand
And see a fiery madness, that would blast
God's miracle of freedom, kindling fast."

   He fix'd a dark, wild look
On his celestial watcher, as in hate ;
 Then grasp'd him, till his passionless grandeur
  shook,
And mutter'd : " Spirit, see the fate of fate
I've left upon mortality's estate.

And thou didst suffer all this ruin, thou
Whose office was to warn me ; 'tis too late
    For me to give thee these reproaches now,
For I am growing cold—my deeds are done,
And thou shouldst blush for them, thou guilty one.

                    " I tell thee, thou shalt hear—
For, Guardian Angel of the Years, I swear
    Thou art a traitor to thy God !   And fear
A traitor's fate, if thou again shalt dare
Neglect thy task.   Then aid him who shall bear
    The sceptre I resign to quench all wrong,
And kindle right—or, when I meet thee where
    None may evade the truth, my oath, as strong
As aught except thy brother Lucifer's curse,
Shall drag thee down to share his doom or worse !

                    " Mortals, I go, I go.
Yet, though we part, it is to meet again ;
    My ghost will come with noiseless step and slow
Along the twilights, whispering of my reign ;
And, in the night-times, oft a mystic strain
    Shall strike your sleep, and ye shall know my tone,
Singing remembered airs, not all in vain,
    And chorus them with an unconscious moan ;

A YEAR.

And I must witness of you in the day
When earth and heaven shall melt in fire away."

      He drew the dark around
His ghastly face—the nations sigh'd farewell ;
  He stagger'd from his throne—an awful sound
Rolled down from every system's every bell,
That toll'd together once to make his knell,
  And the resplendent crown-star, that had flash'd
On the lone Angel's brow, grew black and fell—
  Shattering among six thousand more it crash'd.
I ask'd : "How many stay for him to wear ?"
I woke : and Midnight's silence fill'd the air.

A FALLING STAR.

Just then, upon its wings of fire,
    A star went flying by,
And vanish'd o'er the waves of cloud,
    A sea-bird of the sky!

To-night there ring within my heart
    Old half-forgotten chimes,
Whose mournful music memory caught
    Among its nursery-rhymes.

In those sweet years I've heard them say
    No wish could be in vain,
If it were form'd while flash'd thro' Heaven
    A meteor's sudden train.

Ah, then I only wish'd to catch
    The blue-birds on the hill,
Or, with bare feet to wander down
    Some shady woodland rill.

A FALLING STAR.

For (oh, how long ago it seems !)
  I then was but a child,
Whose cheek was bright, whose golden hair
  Upon the winds flew wild ;

Whose tiny hand drove humming-birds
  From many a rose's breast,
Whose sunny brow and lisping lip
  A mother's kisses press'd.

But since the years have pass'd and left
  Their paleness on my brow,
Their twilight shadows in my heart—
  What are my wishes now ?

When next a fire shall flash along
  The night's eternal blue,
What can I ask ere it shall fade
  Forever from my view ?

MY WEDDING RING.

My heart stirr'd with its golden thrill
   And flutter'd closer up to thine,
In that blue morning of the June
   When first it clasp'd thy love and mine.

In it I see the little room,
   Rose-dim and hush'd with lilies still,
Where the old silence of my life
   Turn'd into music with " I will."

Oh, I would have my folded hands
   Take it into the dust with me :
All other little things of mine
   I'd leave in the bright world with thee.

12   132

A NIGHT AND MORNING—1862-3.

O Memory, the fountains of thy Deep
  Are broken up, and all its fairy shells
Lie glimmering after each dim billow's sweep:
  Once we but saw the rose-bloom in their cells,
And melody was in the sounds alone;
We see the pallor now, and hear the moan.

Our images lie broken in the sand,
  Our blossoms wither'd in the mist, we say;
Our summer birds have left the snowy land,
  Phantoms of tropic songs, and flown away;
Our gorgeous buds have borne no golden fruit;
Our desert's singing springs are dry and mute.

Sweet souls have gone above the awful stars,
  Tired hearts are heavy in the dark below;
The world is blasted with the breath of wars,
  And Heaven folds close the Secret we would know;
Blind shapes of storm move in the gloom, and where
Is the white wing of Calm to light the air?

A NIGHT AND MORNING.

Weird Something, crown'd with bloody asphodels,
  In whose dark watch twelve moons dropp'd faded
     light,
We see thy red path mark'd with bursted shells,
  And ghosts of cannon-thunder haunt the night;
Thy sword has done its work, but work remains:
The victory waits for other ghastly plains.

Like Memnon, singing in old legend, we
  Have given to the setting light our sighs:
Great Angel of the Mystery to be!
  Help us to hail its unveil'd glory rise,
And lay the beauty of a faith divine,
The soul's myrrh-offering, on its morning shrine.

And if when its last sun is gone we moan
  Slow, tremulous dirges full of broken sound;
If whiter images are overthrown;
  If Time's most kingly hopes are yet uncrown'd;
If fiercer signs glare on the walls of Fate—
We know that God is God, and Man can wait.

THE DOVE AND THE ANGEL.

THE roses and stars were in blossom :
　　She leant by the lattice alone,
And a pet dove, white as a lily,
　　Flew out of the night with a moan,
And nestled down close in her bosom,
　　To hide from the wound in its own.

Tears rain'd on the snow of its plumage,
　　Tears rain'd on the golden moonshine ;
" Ah, beautiful, tremulous darling,"
　　She murmured, " my life is like thine—
Only I have no bosom to fly to,
　　My bird, as you fly into mine."

The south-moon dropp'd under the shadow,
　　Yet she stay'd to remember and weep,
Till—what was the wonderful Presence,
　　So quiet and holy and deep,
That stole thro' the dreams of the roses,
　　Till they shook out their sweetness in sleep？

THE DOVE AND THE ANGEL.

Ah, an Angel that once was a mortal
  Flew out of the glories unknown,
And, like the white dove from the darkness
  That came to her love with its moan,
She nestled down close in his bosom,
  And hid from the wound in her own.

TWO BLUSH-ROSES.

A BLUSH-ROSE lay in the summer ;
   There were golden lights in the sky,
And a woman saw the blossom
   As she stood with her lover nigh.

A band in the flowering distance
   Play'd a dreamy Italian air,
Like a memory changed to music,
   And it drifted everywhere.

'T was an exiled love of its Southland,
   That air, and its delicate wails
Were only the wandering echoes
   Of the songs of nightingales.

"I love you," he tenderly whisper'd ;
   "I love you," she answer'd as low :
And the music grew sweeter and sweeter,
   Because it had listen'd, I know.

TWO BLUSH-ROSES.

But she look'd at the rose in the summer,
   And said, with a tremulous tear,
"The love that now beats in my bosom
   Will bloom in a blush-rose next year."

A blush-rose lay in the summer;
   There were golden lights in the sky,
And a woman saw the blossom—
   As she stood with her lover nigh.

The band in the flowering distance
   Play'd the dreamy Italian air,
Like a memory changed to music,
   And it drifted everywhere.

"I love you," he tenderly whisper'd;
   "I love you," she timidly said:
And the music grew sadder and sadder,
   And the blush-rose before them dropp'd dead.

Then he knew that the music remember'd,
   And knew the love that had beat
Last year in her beautiful bosom
   Lay dead in the rose at his feet.

ON A WEDDING DAY.

I LOOK far-off across the blue,
  Still distance vague with woods and Spring—
The Earth is sweet with buds and dew;
  The birds their early carols sing.

I look, and somehow wish the hours
  Held calm and sun and bloom alone:
No fallen leaves, no wither'd flowers,
  No storm, no wreck, no mist, no moan;

No painted palms of air on sand,
  No poisons where the spice-winds blow,
No dark shapes haunting sea and land—
  But wherefore am I dreaming so?

It is because this music swells
  Across the lighted April day—
Because I hear your bridal bells,
  Fair girl, a thousand miles away.

139

ON A WEDDING DAY.

Yes, lovely in a holy place,
   Enchanted by my dream you rise :
The young blush-roses on your face,
   The timid darkness in your eyes.

And, golden on your hand, I see
   The glitter of a sacred thing :
I wish some Fairy, friend, may be
   Slave of the ring—your wedding ring

HOME AGAIN.

IT is a mournful thing to have no home!—
  To wear a shroud of loneliness on earth,
To know that fate has forced thee forth to roam,
  And fear thyself unwelcome by each hearth;
To hear harsh, stranger voices and to raise
A drooping lid and meet a loveless gaze!

Once, long ago, the lightning's quivering glare
  Lit the strange sadness of a boyish face,
And vanish'd from bright waves of tangled hair
  That seem'd to touch the dark with sunny grace,
While the sad wind with many a fond caress
Sigh'd for a kindred wanderer's loneliness.

Weary and wretched he had sunk to sleep
  Ere sunset's crimson loveliness was gone;
The twilight came and passed—night's gloom grew
    deep
  In the damp forest—still he slumbered on,

141

HOME AGAIN.

And—oh! how strange!—that friendless mourner
    smiled
As calmly as a cradled, thoughtless child.

Ah! Memory bore him to his home; he heard
    The murmur'd music of his childish hours,
He saw familiar trees and each bright bird
    Whose sweet song gush'd at spring-time mid
        the flowers;
His sister smiled, his mother's thrilling kiss
Flush'd his pale cheek with more than former
    bliss.

He woke while listening for the words of love,
    And heard the passing night-wind's deep fare-
        well!
He saw the trees around, the clouds above,
    And murmur'd, starting from that blessèd spell,
" O God! the loved are gone—my dream is o'er;
This is a forest—I've a home no more!"

World-wanderer, thou art in a forest too!
    Oh! dream and smile as did that lonely boy—
There is a home for thee; the loved, the true,
    Await thee there amid unfading joy;

HOME AGAIN.

Weary and sad thou too shalt fall asleep—
The shades around thee will be dim and deep!

Angels shall bear thee to thy home, and thou
   Wilt wake amid the light of early years;
Thy mother's real kiss shall thrill thy brow
   And still the quivering of earth's lingering fears
Remember'd voices with an added strain
Of trembling love will whisper Home Again!

OF A PARTING.

UNDER a calm of stars, my own,
  Under a drooping crescent light,
You go, while fairy sounds are blown
Out of the dreams of winds, my own—
  You go across the night ;
But on some far-off strand of sunrise
  Our hearts meet in a radiant bliss,
                Not damp, like this !

You go ; the calm of stars must go,
  The crescent light, the fairy sounds ;
Billows of cloud will overflow
The golden skies : but you must go.
  And in its stormy rounds
The dark will hear low, fluttering voices
  Cry in my heart, like lonesome birds,
                For your sweet words.

You go, and twilights made for love
  Will gloom between us, dim with dew ;
The spring-loosed music of the dove
Will search the emerald woods for love,

And I will long for you,
Among the blue and pearly blossoms
   Far on the mossy hills, alone,
        My own, my own.

But you must loose my hands and go ._
   Haste with those tremulous words of pain,
For I, most loved of all, I know
(The thought is full of tears) some go
   And never come again;
So wait, and let me look forever
   Into the tenderness that lies
        In those deep eyes.

Ah! you are gone; and I—I hold
   My vacant arms to all who part,
And weep for them, and long to fold
Those strangers close, and say: " I hold
   Your sorrow in my heart;"
But look—the calm of stars is o'er us,
   And we go toward their lighted shore,
        And part no more.

1861.

AN EAGLE'S PLUME FROM PALESTINE.

LEAVING the summer in the palms asleep
For lonely circles in the upper deep—
   Leaving the wild crusader's risen blood,
   That stands in many a crimson-stainéd bud,
As if to make a gentle guard of flowers,
   To keep the memory of the Holy Cross
Safe from the dark hands of unholy powers—
   Leaving the valley lilies and the moss :
Far up the silence of that Eastern sky,
   Whose suns and stars are haunted by the shine
   Left by the death-smile of a God, 'twas thine
To feel the vastness of infinity !

Phantoms of olive-trees, old cedar glooms,
A sacred stream—with tremulous, snowy plumes
   Bearing the Father's blessing from above,
   Shaped in the timid likeness of a dove—
And many solemn things, before me sweep,
   Call'd up by thee, thou that hast sailed far noons,
And lain against a lonesome mountain sleep
   Close to the golden-lighted Asian moons;

AN EAGLE'S PLUME FROM PALESTINE.

Yet, dusk enchanter, saddest of the sights,
  Which thy still wizardry has come to bring,
  Seems the dread picture of a falling wing—
A flying farewell to the sunward heights!

A falling wing—ah, even when it glows
With little fires and burns down from a rose,
  It must resist its sinking, with a pain
  That is sublime—a wish to rise again:
But when its place has been above the cloud,
  Where its high strength has dared the storm afar,
Then feels a downward weakness, slow and proud
  It drops—as grandly as an unsphered star,
Whose arms of light strive with their utmost powers
  To hold a place in heaven; and thus dropp'd thine,
  Dead eagle of the skies of Palestine,
And thus drop many in this world of ours!

A BIRD'S WING AND A SOUL'S.

FOR MY SISTER AND BROTHER.

THIS small bright wing, that used to fly
  In far Kentucky's summer light
And lift clear music toward the sky,
  Lies full of tears to-night.

Wild little memory of the woods
  In whose dark paths we loved to go,
When the old hills were flush'd with buds
  Or pallid with the snow:

I kiss you, tenderly and fast—
  For her, the beautiful and dear,
Between whose lips and mine have pass'd
  The dim waves of a year;

For him through whose dark, careless hair
  The shadows of the palms now play—
Perchance in warm Pacific air
  He thinks of us to-day.

A BIRD'S WING AND A SOUL'S.

Ah, were I but the light, free bird
   That wore you through old woodland glooms,
Familiar leaves should soon be stirr'd
   With my returning plumes.

But that wild, wingéd thing is dust
   Where wither'd falls have dropp'd and blown,
And my wild, wingéd thoughts, I trust,
   Can fly on love alone.

THE CHILD IN THE STREET.

EVEN as a tender parent lovingly
   Sends a dear child in some true servant's care
   Forth on the street, for larger light and air,
Feeling the sun her guardian will be,
And dreaming with a blushful pride that she
   Will earn sweet smiles and glances everywhere,
   From loving faces, and that passers fair
Will bend and bless and kiss her, when they see,
And ask her name and if her home is near,
   And think, " O gentle child, how bless'd are they
   Whose twofold love bears up a single flower !"
And so with softer musing move away :
   We send thee forth, O Book, thy little hour—
The world may pardon us to hold thee dear.

Pol

Check Out More Titles From HardPress Classics Series In this collection we are offering thousands of classic and hard to find books. This series spans a vast array of subjects — so you are bound to find something of interest to enjoy reading and learning about.

Subjects:
Architecture
Art
Biography & Autobiography
Body, Mind &Spirit
Children & Young Adult
Dramas
Education
Fiction
History
Language Arts & Disciplines
Law
Literary Collections
Music
Poetry
Psychology
Science
…and many more.

Visit us at www.hardpress.net